SCOTLAND
THE GRAVE

SCOTLAND'S
GHASTLY
GHOSTS

CHARLES SINCLAIR

GOBLINSHEAD

MAR -- 2012

First published 2011
© Martin Coventry & Joyce Miller 2011

Published by
GOBLINSHEAD

130B Inveresk Road, Musselburgh EH21 7AY, Scotland
t: 0131 665 2894 e: goblinshead@sol.co.uk

British Library Cataloguing in Publication Data
A catalogue record for this book is available from
the British Library.

ISBN 978 1899874 52 1

Typeset by GOBLINSHEAD
Printed and bound in Scotland by Bell & Bain

Disclaimer:
The information contained in this *Scotland's Ghastly Ghosts* (the
"Material") is believed to be accurate at the time of printing, but no
representation or warranty is given (express or implied) as to its
accuracy, completeness or correctness. The author and publisher do not
accept any liability whatsoever for any direct, indirect or consequential
loss or damage arising in any way from any use of or reliance on this
Material for any purpose.

While every care has been taken to compile and check all the
information in this book, it is possible that mistakes may have occurred.
If you know of any corrections, alterations or improvements, please
contact the author or the publishers at the address above.

Contents

Introduction

This book is about ghastly ghosts. In Scotland there are hundreds of places which are said to be haunted, probably many more than a thousand. And while many of the stories of wicked bogles and sinister spectres are indeed quite ghastly, it should also be mentioned that many ghosts are seemingly gentle and never do anyone any harm; indeed, often it is their death which is the most ghastly part of the haunting, and that was meted out by the living, not by the dead or their uneasy spirits.

Gathered together here are simply some of the most ghastly ghosts: the headless horseman of the MacLaines and the ghostly drummer of Cortachy and the evils spirits that afflicted Glenluce, Galdenoch or Ringcroft of Stocking and the unexplained goings on in the vaults or streets under Edinburgh are indeed quite ghastly and would make anyone go a little pale. Then there are also skeletons buried under the floor, or the inn where guests have woken up in bed with what they thought was the wet corpse of a drowned child.

Other manifestations are more interesting than gruesome: the hot kiss of a flirtatious phantom at Meggernie or the ghost that may have carved its name fifty-foot up into the window sill of Fyvie Castle (on the wedding night of her former husband) or the phantom cannon ball that repeatedly seemed to smash through a window.

So, do ghosts exist?

This is impossible to answer, despite much research. Although hundreds of places are said to be haunted, evidence for the existence of ghosts remains as insubstantial as the phantoms themselves, if verbal testimony of witnesses is excluded. Certain television programmes about haunted locations may leave some watchers thinking that supernatural activity – and especially violent activity – is very common, so common that all that is needed is a team of celebrities and a camera and all hell breaks loose. This is, however, far from the case. Even complicated and intensive psychic investigations of sites rarely unearth anything of substance.

The stories in this book are gathered and pieced together from a variety of different sources: books, pamphlets, guides, newspaper articles and contact with the owners of the sites. By no means all people who live in supposedly haunted places acknowledge either the ghost or the story. And it is simply impossible to verify the veracity of accounts from Victorian times or later or to sometimes distinguish the folkloric element from the actual account. For example, all female ghosts are described as being beautiful, despite there being few reliable instances of them being observed. It could be concluded that only beautiful young women become ghosts, leaving their plain sisters no doubt somewhat relieved, but this seems unlikely.

While ghastly ghosts can make a visit to a place more interesting, it should be remembered that many of these stories are hundreds of years old. People lived in reputedly haunted houses without any particular problems, except the odd shiver now and again and something to discuss over the dinner table when the house bogle was feeling especially restless. With two exceptions, there are no stories about ghosts physically hurting people.

The first exception is the three cases from the seventeenth century regarding what, might be called, poltergeist activity, covered in the chapter in this book called Evil Spirits. Even in these, it would appear nobody was seriously injured.

The second exception is ghost tours in Edinburgh, where a variety of physical attacks, including scratches and things been thrown and even deaths, have been reported on walking tours in Greyfriars Kirkyard and elsewhere. This seems incredible. Firstly, that a ghost would be able to do this, secondly that any guide would take people on a tour where they could be seriously injured or even die.

If books about ghosts caused similar damage, they would be banned…

At the end of the book websites and phone numbers are listed for the reader who is interested in visiting sites open to the public or going to hotels or hostelries.

The stories in this book are (hopefully) interesting, intriguing, scary – and even a little ghastly – but not really quite enough to make the reader *dead* scared.

Charles Sinclair
May 2011

The Meggernie Haunting: A Ghost of Two Halves

'I was awakened in the night by what appeared to be a burning kiss, it appeared to scorch the flesh through the cheek bone. I jumped up in bed and distinctly saw the upper half body of a Lady pass from the side of my bed, go along the room and through the door that was screwed up, as if going into Beau's room.'

So wrote Reverend E. J. Simmons in a letter of the 7th of January 1882 about his ghostly encounter at Meggernie Castle in Perthshire.

Meggernie Castle.

1

Simmons and his friend, Beaumont Featherstone (who wrote a similar letter about his experiences in January 1883), had visited the castle around twelve or thirteen years previously (1869 or 1870) when the castle was owned by Mr Herbert Wood, a friend of Featherstone.

According to letters from the two visitors, they claimed to have heard no rumours or tales of ghostly sightings prior to their visit. They were to be housed in two large bedrooms in the original tower as the rest of the accommodation in the castle was occupied. There was a connecting door through a closet between the two rooms which could not be opened. Simmons and Featherstone were in a party visiting the Highlands of Scotland for shooting – particularly grouse – and fishing and all things 'Scotch', all of which were very popular during the Victorian era. Simmons wrote that he was delighted with his room as it had windows to the north and south, giving him views over the park land to the mountains beyond. Both men went to their respective rooms after a tiring day and Simmons fell asleep quickly only to be woken in the wee small hours by the ghost's hot and painful kiss.

Simmons's account noted that the apparition appeared to pass through the door to Featherstone's room but he '... jumped out of bed and went at once to the door and tried it. It was as firm as a lock ...'. He then checked his cheek, expecting to find it blistered from the hot kiss, but there was no mark, although it ached as if it was burnt. At that time Simmons did not call on his friend or awaken any of the other guests or members of the household, but instead, with his trusty lamp in his hand, in the manner of all worthy Victorian explorers, went to the stairs outside his room in search of the mysterious apparition. When he found no evidence of either a corporeal or spiritual visitor, he returned, somewhat wearily, to his bed feeling 'cold and uncomfortable'.

In the morning when the two friends woke, it transpired that Simmons was not alone in experiencing a broken night's sleep. According to Simmons, Featherstone reported that he too had had a terrible night and his account has him being woken by the ghost which then disappeared into the closet; he also noticed that the apparition had a beautiful face, but one that was spoiled by a 'look of despair'.

At breakfast, where the guests would convene over a leisurely hour or two, Simmons was keen to regale his exciting news but 'a look from Mrs Herbert Wood stopped me, for she was afraid it would alarm her guests'. The two men then appear to have reported their nocturnal experience to their hosts as, according to Simmons, they were told about a previous female guest who had disturbed the whole household by wakening everybody in the middle of the night complaining that she had felt a woman lying down beside her. Also a servant girl, working in the kitchen, had claimed to have seen the lower half of a woman walking along the passage. It was said that a similar apparition had been seen several times, covered in blood, either beside an avenue of lime trees in the castle's parkland or in the local graveyard.

Featherstone left the castle quite soon after but Simmons stayed on for several more days, although he had been moved to a different bedroom. About ten days later, while he was sitting writing in one of the other rooms, the heavy, iron-studded oak door opened and the room became icy cold. As he walked along a passage, he had another ghostly encounter and noticed the apparition of the same face, which he had seen in his bedroom, looking in through a window.

In his 1882 letter about the experience, Simmons mentioned that the local servants would not stay in the old part of the castle and refused to go near the graveyard at night, as there had been many sightings of a female apparition, walking or sitting around the gravestones. Indeed Simmons seems to have tried to do some research amongst the local community who appeared reluctant to elaborate – or repeat old stories to strangers: 'The people seemed to dislike talking on the subject extensively and looked angered when questioned about it'. Despite this lack of communication, Simmons was able to suggest that the origins of the sightings may have related to a legend about one of the Menzies lairds of Meggernie, who murdered his young wife in a fit of jealous rage.

Meggernie Castle, in the picturesque Glen Lyon, is an imposing sixteenth-century tower house located to the north of Killin in Perthshire. It was one of several strongholds built by Colin Campbell of Glen Lyon, one of the branches of the very powerful

Campbell clan. In later years the property passed to Menzies of Culdares and the murderous legend relates to one of this family.

One of the lairds, the date is not specific, married a particularly attractive and younger bride. Although there were no tales of infidelity, Menzies was unable to trust his wife and his jealousy grew to such an extent that he was unable to trust or believe anything she did or said. Actions were interpreted as suspicious until finally he snapped and attacked and murdered the poor woman. In an attempt to conceal the deed, and delay any punishment, Menzies cut the corpse in two and hid her remains under the floor or in a closet in one of the rooms in the tower, depending on the version of the story. This room later became known as the 'haunted room'. Menzies then informed his staff and other inquirers that his wife was visiting relatives and that they then intended to make a trip to the continent and would be away for some time. The castle was shut up and it was several months before Menzies returned with the sad news that his wife had drowned during their visit to Europe.

Menzies then seems to have tried to bury his wife's remains, which would not have been a particularly pleasant task as the corpse would have certainly been in a decayed and rotting condition after several months in a chest or closet. He buried the bottom half in the graveyard, but the disposal of the upper half of her torso was less successful as by whatever means, naturally, accidentally or on purpose, Menzies perished himself before he moved it. He was found dead one morning in the tower; some suggest that he may have died of a heart attack after the exertions of moving the corpse, that he may have fallen, that he was murdered by his wife's suspicious relatives – or that he was frightened to death by the apparition of his murdered wife.

According to legend, it was from that point that strange manifestations began to be recorded, and that the apparition had two parts: the top half of a woman in the upper rooms in the tower and the lower half, wearing a blood-splattered dress, seen on the ground floor, outside in the castle grounds, or in the graveyard.

The Simmons/Featherstone accounts seem to have been similar to other, later, versions. The wife of a Colonel Kinloch Grant, who had been staying at the castle one autumn, reported waking in the night to see the apparition of a woman bending over her. In 1928 Dr Douglas MacKay from Aberfeldy, who was staying in one of the lower rooms in the old tower, claimed to have heard footsteps outside his room and saw the upper part of the apparition floating near the ceiling, which emitted a pink glow.

During renovation work on the castle in the early years of the twentieth century, it is said that the upper bones of a skeleton were discovered beneath the floor in one of the upper chambers, and, although the remains were buried, hauntings and manifestations continued to be reported, including banging and knockings. It is thought a rapping sound heralded an appearance of the ghost.

Meggernie Castle: the old tower.

Simmons's letter emphasised that he was not superstitious, that he found the old tower charming, and enjoyed the novelty of the whole castle, despite the original part being gloomy. Featherstone, in his letter, seemed less romantic about the whole event than his friend; indeed he was a little defensive, as he wrote, 'I don't care about talking about it to anyone and I hate writing about it and never have before, as I don't like being laughed at for the reason that it [was] not tosh'.

He recounted that he was awoken, around 2.30 in the morning, by a pink light and saw a female standing at the foot of his bed. His initial reaction was that it must have been the housekeeper: it was not uncommon for domestic staff to appear in guests' bedrooms in the middle of the night but usually it would be by some prior, secret, arrangement for a completely different type of assignation! Featherstone described how the ghost came alongside his bed and leaned over him, but when he sat up the apparition retreated into the closet or cupboard that was in the thickness of the wall of the room (and connected to Simmons's room). He then took a light and followed in to the tiny closet where he saw nothing but a towel rail. Looking under the bed, he found nothing and he then spent some hours trying to get back to sleep. He noted that in the morning Simmons looked 'most unfortunate' and that that was when he heard Simmons's account of the hot, burning kiss. Both men noted that the ghost they had seen was only the apparition of an upper torso – neither saw any legs.

Featherstone admitted that he never slept in the old tower again, although he seems to have enjoyed the grouse shooting, which was the main purpose of their visit: they must have been at the castle some time between 12th August and 10th December. In his letter he also noted that recently he had met at a hotel a nameless 'lady' who had been at Meggernie and who had also seen the ghost. He claimed that she described it just as Featherstone had seen it, down to the expression on the face and the way the hair was done.

It may be, of course, that the two men collaborated and concocted the whole story, but their ghostly encounters certainly contributed to – or perhaps created – an enduring local legend

The Ghostly Drummer of Cortachy Castle

Many noble families in Scotland have their own heralds of death, the appearance of a ghost or sometimes some other kind of event which predicts a death. These are akin to the Irish banshee (banshee means 'fairy woman' in Gaelic), which would be heard shrieking when a member of family was close to death or disaster was to come. In Scotland many castles and great houses had spirits known as gruagach, commonly now known as Green Ladies, who would be seen weeping if misfortune was to strike, but would also laugh to presage good tidings.

Other portentous events recorded are the appearance of an animal: a white stag among the Hamilton Earls of Arran, a ram (known as the 'Doom of Airlie Castle') for the Ogilvy Earls of Airlie (also see below), a robin for the inhabitants of Pitcaple Castle, and a swan with a red breast for Kirkpatricks of Closeburn, the howling of a hound at Barnbougle Castle. In several places a bell is reputed to toll by itself. One story concerns the MacCullochs of Myrton. A ship transporting the bell and pulpit of Kirkmaiden Church across Luce Bay foundered and sank. Afterwards, a bell could be heard from the depths of the sea when one of the family was to perish; similar tales about the toll of a bell concern Abergeldie Castle, Coull and Craigdarroch House.

Two of the creepiest stories, however, regard

Cortachy Castle and its ghostly drummer, and the headless horseman of the MacLaines of Lochbuie on Mull (the next chapter).

Located about four miles north of the town of Kirriemuir in Angus, Cortachy Castle is an impressive and imposing country house, which incorporates an ancient castle within the present walls. Cortachy has long been the property of the Ogilvy Earls of Airlie, and the building dates from the fifteenth century. The castle was sacked by the Earl of Argyll in 1641, was visited by Charles II six years later, but was then torched by Oliver Cromwell's forces soon afterwards. Following their involvement in the Jacobite Risings, the Ogilvys were forfeited and their titles stripped, and they did not recover the Earldom of Airlie until 1796, fifty years after culmination of the crushing of the Rising at the Battle of Culloden. The Earls still own Cortachy and the gardens are open to the public once a year.

The events go back more than one hundred

Cortachy Castle.

and fifty years. A guest staying at Cortachy Castle early in the spring of 1845 was Miss Margaret Dalrymple, who was accompanied by her companion, Mrs Ann Day, on a two-day visit. They arrived late in the evening and Miss Dalrymple was given her room in the ancient part of the house and then had to hurry to dress in time for dinner. Her host was the then Earl, David Ogilvy, who at that time, was married to his second wife, Margaret Bruce of Cowden – his first wife had died ten years earlier. The Earl was not in especially good health during the visit.

As she sat resting on a sofa in her chamber before dinner, Miss Dalrymple heard – as if directly beneath the floor – the sound of bagpipes and then, following that, the distinct beating of a drum.

Going down to dinner, and not suspecting anything might be amiss, she remarked to the Earl,

'What is that strange music you have about the house? You assuredly have an excellent piper?'

The Earl dropped his cutlery and retired from the table, and did not reappear, going to library and eating there. Other diners were confused.

The following day, Mrs Ann Day was alone in Miss Dalrymple's chamber. She later recounted:

> 'The next morning, whilst the family were at breakfast, I was quite alone in Miss Dalrymple's room, and as I stood up from the fire I heard, as I thought, a carriage drive up, and stop dead,

directly under my feet. Immediately there followed the sound of another carriage drawing up, and stopping in exactly the same manner. And then, as if following the vehicles, came the tramp, tramp, tramp of marching soldiers. Then I heard some shrill notes of the instrument so distinctly that I looked round instinctively, expecting to see the piper in the room. In another moment I was more startled by the beating of a drum. About this there was something indescribably weird and disagreeable; it seemed as the drummer was making his way through the floor.

'Being a perfect stranger to the place, I thought there might be a coach-road and an entrance-door to the castle, near the room in which I stood, and that some distinguished guests were arriving or departing.

'On looking out of the window, however, I found there was no door nor coach-road near, and not a human being was to be seen. I concluded, therefore, that the sounds must have been echoed from a distance.

'The next morning, before our departure, Lady Airlie came to the door of Miss Dalrymple's room, to give her a £5 note for an orphan school in which she was interested. Neither of us ever saw the Countess again. She was confined of twins at Brighton some months afterwards and died. It was not until Miss Dalrymple, a few days after we left the castle, asked me if I had heard 'the strange music there,' that I disclosed my experience; and then for the first time I learned from her the tradition about the Airlie drummer-boy. She told me that she herself had been totally in ignorance of it, until her allusion at the dinner-table of the music she had heard elicited from another guest an explanation.'

The reason, of course, that the Earl was so disturbed by Miss Dalrymple's announcement of piping and drumming was that this was not the first time it had been heard. Indeed, some years earlier, in 1835, the Earl himself had been staying with friends in England. While sitting in the garden, he had heard what he thought was a marching band, and had said so to the lady of the house. She reported hearing no such music, although he could still do so, including the thump of a drum.

The Earl realised that, according to family tradition, this might be the music that heralded a death in his family. The following day he learned of the death of his then wife, Clementina Graham of Duntrune, who had died unexpectedly because of a premature birth. At the time of Miss Dalrymple's visit, the Earl suspected that the phantom music might presage his own death but indeed he lived for a further four years.

The Countess of Airlie, Margaret Bruce, died in June of 1845 at Brighton during childbirth (she had twins, one of whom also died), which was some months after the manifestation of the phantom drummer. The Countess apparently believed the drummer had come for her, according to one author, writing:

> 'I have heard that a paper was found in her desk after her death, declaring her conviction that the drum was for her; and it has been suggested that probably the thing preyed upon her mind and caused the catastrophe; but in the first place, from the mode of her death, that does not appear to be the case; in the second, even if it were, the fact of the verification of the prognostic remains unaffected; beside which, those who insist upon taking refuge in the hypothesis are bound to admit, that before people living in the world, like Lord and Lady Airlie, could attach so much importance to the prognostic as to entail such fatal effects, they must have had very good reason for believing in it.'

Nor was that the last time the drummer was heard. On the evening of 19th August 1849, a young

Englishman was on his way to Tulchan of Glenisla, a plain shooting lodge in the remote, rugged but picturesque Glen Isla. Tulchan was also a property of the Earls of Airlie, and is located some twenty miles north and west of Kirriemuir, also in Angus.

The name of the young Englishmen is not recorded, unfortunately, but he was riding along with a local men to the lodge, having already covered a score of miles or so. At around half past eight, they had spied the house and were glad that their journey was almost over. The Englishman, however, heard music, what he thought was a brass band, coming from a low ridge of ground in front of him. The music rather came and went on the wind, having an unearthly and eerie character, and the young man was surprised that a band might be found in such a remote location as there were no other houses near Tulchan.

Realising that his companion could not hear the sounds, the young man quizzed the local man, but his only response was that the music was 'no canny', spurring his mount onwards.

The young Englishman finally arrived at the lodge to find that his host, the future Earl of Airlie, had been called away to London because of the illness of his father. And that there were no musicians, either at the building or in the vicinity. He told other guests about hearing the eerie music, having no knowledge of the legend, and was told,

'I fear the sound you have heard bodes no good, for there is an ancient legend that when the Head of the House of Airlie is about to die a band plays outside his house in Scotland.'

The next day, the 20th of August, the then Earl of Airlie died in Regent Langham Place in London.

So what is the legend of the drummer of Cortachy? There are at least three versions of the tale behind the haunting. One is that in life the drummer failed to warn the Ogilvys when their castle was about to be attacked. Another tells that the man was romantically entangled, or so the Earl thought anyway, with the Earl's wife. Either way, the poor man was forced into his own drum and then cast off the battlements from the old part of the building (in which Miss Margaret Dalrymple was lodging when she heard the music). Just before he died, he cursed the family, warning them he would be heard playing as a herald of bad news. A third version is that he was burnt to death here in 1645 after being taken as a hostage.

The drummer is also said to have been heard at Achnacarry, and even abroad in South Africa.

The next Earl, another David Ogilvie, died in 1881 in New Mexico in the USA. This time two of his relatives heard drumming, although at Achnacarry, near Spean Bridge in the Highlands of Scotland (and nowhere near Cortachy), on the 25th of September 1881. An account was written down by Lady Margaret Cameron of Locheil, whose family owned (and owns) Achnacarry.

> 'After dinner I left the drawing room to get out a piece of china to show my

sister-in-law, then Lady Dalkeith; and to the Countess of Lathom, then Lady Skelmersdale. On returning to the room both became silent; I noticed the fact but made no remark. Two days after, on Tuesday I think, on the arrival of the post, my sister-in-law, Lady Dalkeith, came to my room with newspaper in her hand and asked me first if there was any tradition about curious noises or sounds being heard in the family? On my answering her there was not, she asked if I had noticed Lady Skelmersdale's and her silence on my return to the drawing-room two nights before? I replied in the affirmative. Then she told me that, while I was out of the room, she and Lady Skelmersdale distinctly heard the sound of a drummer beating the drum outside the house and remarked how it sounded like what they had heard described as 'The Airlie Drummer'; but decided not to mention the subject for fear of alarming me in case there should be any tradition in the Locheil family. She then told me the death of Lord Airlie was announced in the paper as having taken place in America, the same night that she and Lady Skelmersdale had heard the sound.'

The Earl died of a fever and double

pneumonia on the 25th. One explanation why the drummer might have been heard at Achnacarry is that he had been from the Cameron clan.

The drumming also apparently presaged the death of the then Countess of Airlie in 1884, and then the death of the next Earl (yet another David) in 1900, during fighting in the Boer War in South Africa. The Earl was a colonel in the Twelfth Lancers but was shot through the heart on the 11th of June at Diamond Hill in the Transvaal. The previous day was a Sunday, and Boer prisoners had complained about a band playing on the Sabbath, while other troops reported hearing a drum thumping away.

There are no tales that the ghostly drummer of Cortachy has been heard since. It should also be said that the stories surrounding the Airlie family were well known and featured in many newspapers, not least the *Daily Telegraph,* with long and detailed articles.

Perhaps the most alarming of all the portents of death is that of the MacLaine clan, who for hundreds of years held the lands of Lochbuie to the south of the island of Mull in the Western Isles. That story is covered in the next chapter.

The Headless Horseman of the MacLaines

'The mist has fallen, rolling down the mountains, eating up the world, chill against the face. Lochbuie is shrouded in dank grey. Quiet, still, a formless world, without feature, lost. The only respite from the grey, the road runs into the clouds, before and after. Noises echo in that dreary mist. The rumble of hooves, the clink of harness, the creak of saddle, approaches, rapidly. A galloping horse, riding without heed. A darker shadow speeding closer. Now an upright rider, on a great dun-coloured horse. The horsemen clad in a flowing green cloak, stooped it seems. Shadowed by a ferocious dog. Thundering on. And on. Then clear, for a moment, the rider headless, galloping through the clouds, the glen full of thunder and horseman and fear. Then swallowed in the grey. Just a dark shadow, receding. Only the rumble of hooves to be heard. Then nothing again. The grey mist.

'And death and misfortune to come.'

Moy Castle, Lochbuie.

Few places in Scotland (or indeed Europe) are quite as beautiful as Lochbuie, which lies to the south of the Hebridean island of Mull. By the sandy shore is the stark Moy Castle, the plain and ruinous tower of the MacLaines of Lochbuie, still standing guard in a fantastic unspoilt spot, overlooked by the glowering mountain of Ben Buie. The old castle was replaced by a mansion, itself replaced by the present eighteenth-century Lochbuie House. Few places are as beautiful – and few places have such a grim ghost story.

To the north of Lochbuie, and cutting into Mull from east to west, runs the great valley of Glen Mor, through which the main road runs from the ferry point at Craignure, and from the MacLeans' great stronghold of Duart Castle, across the island to end eventually at the crossing point to Iona. A few miles west of Strathcoil in Glen Mor is a small lochan known as Loch Sguabain, and at the north end is an islet, marked on the Ordnance Survey map as a crannog.

This was, however, the island fortress of Ewan MacLaine, also known as Ewan of the Little Head, whose headless corpse, still upright on a phantom horse, is said to herald death or illness in the chiefs of the MacLaines of Lochbuie.

Ewan was the only son and heir of Iain Og, fifth laird of Lochbuie, and was a renowned warrior. Ewan's wife, known as the Black Swan and a daughter of chief of the MacDougalls of Lorn, was not a happy woman because of the paucity of their marriage settlement. She was accustomed to comfort and the island residence was cold and cramped and Ewan did not have sufficient lands to afford better – nor was she prepared to wait until Iain Og died and Ewan came into his inheritance.

So, reputedly on her prompting, Ewan went to his father to receive at least part of his inheritance, but his father refused point blank. Their dispute escalated and then became violent, Ewan raising a strong force to press his claim, Iain Og aided by the powerful MacLeans of Duart, a related but rival clan. The year was 1538 and nothing could now stop the battle.

On the eve of the fight, Ewan met an old woman (described in one account as being dressed in green) washing bloody shirts, a Bean Nighe (a 'lady of the night' in Gaelic, although not a personage anyone would want to meet as the spirit is a herald

View from Glen More, looking south over Loch Sguabain.

of likely death), and unfortunately for him one of the shirts was his, meaning that he might perish in the coming conflict. The hag told him that if his wife offered him bread and cheese with her own hand, without him asking for it, he would be victorious. The morning came and, unfortunately for Ewan, no bread or cheese was forthcoming.

Nonetheless (although perhaps not hugely optimistic about his prospects), Ewan rode into battle, but at the outset was summarily slain by an axe man standing on a rock. Ewan's head was severed cleanly from his head, but his body stayed rooted upright in his saddle. His mount galloped off down Glen Mor, riding for miles before finally coming to a halt near the northern tip of Loch Sguabain. He was temporarily buried at the place, a stone once marking the spot, before being taken to Iona and there interred near the abbey.

From that day on, however, his headless apparition mounted on a phantom dun-coloured horse was reputedly seen (or just heard), galloping along Glen Mor or at Lochbuie, whenever one of the family of the chiefs of the MacLaines was ill or was about to die. In some tales, the bogle is accompanied by a black hunting dog, and it is said that on an occasion in 1909, when Murdoch MacLaine died, only the dog was seen. Indeed, Lochbuie House was reported as being haunted by a black dog, being both seen and heard, at one time.

One story is that Ewan's ghost has been seen three times in recent times, and has also appeared on the island of Coll. The last recorded occasion was in 1958, on the death of Olive, wife of Kenneth, twenty-fourth of Lochbuie. This was well after the MacLaines sold the majority of the property, including Lochbuie House, although they apparently kept possession of the castle – and of the ghost.

Lillias Drummond and the Ghosts of Fyvie

Many hundreds of places in Scotland are reputedly haunted. Often it is possible to at least guess who (in life) the ghost was: a murder, a suicide, an untimely death, a tragic life indicate the identity, or perhaps from a portrait or a ghost being observed by a loved one or by an acquaintance.

But in one case (if the story is to be believed) at Fyvie Castle, the ghost left proof positive of both its presence and its name. For, some fifty foot above the ground and carved outwards into a window sill, in finely sculpted letters, are the words:

D[ame] LILLIES DRUMMOND

Nor is there any dispute about this part of the ghost story. Fyvie Castle is in the care of The National Trust of Scotland and is open to the public – and a visit to the Drummond Room of the castle will confirm the existence of the writing as described.

So who was Lillias Drummond and why would she haunt Fyvie Castle?

Lillias Drummond was born about 1574, and was the daughter of Patrick Drummond, third Lord Drummond, and Lady Elizabeth Lindsay. She was married to Alexander Seton in 1592, when she was seventeen or eighteen; he was in his mid thirties.

Seton was a man on the way up in James VI's Scotland. He was a judge and Lord President of the Court of Session, commendator (administrator) of Pluscarden Abbey, and then Lord Fyvie from 1598. Fyvie Castle, the seat of the estate and some miles from Turriff in Aberdeenshire in the north-east of Scotland, is a spectacular building, extended down the centuries by a succession of owners (of whom the Setons were neither the first nor the last).

Seton went on to be become Earl of Dunfermline in 1606 and was also Chancellor of Scotland, making him one of the most important men in Scotland. Not that Lillias lived to see either of these last two honours as she was dead by then.

Fyvie Castle.

It could well be that Seton believed that he was creating a dynasty, and for a dynasty a man needs, at least, one son.

There is nothing to suggest that Lillias was not a wife of impeccable character, but unfortunately, although she give birth to four daughters (Anne, Isobel, Margaret and Sophia) who survived into adulthood (another daughter died in infancy and there may have been other miscarriages), she did not produce a son.

Not that she should have been held responsibility for that, of course.

On the 8th of May 1601 Lillias died, at the age of about twenty-seven years old, young even for the turn of the seventeenth century. In some accounts foul play has been suggested – in fact, that Seton deliberately starved Lillias to death – but there is no evidence for this, nor does it seem likely that Lillias's powerful family would not have intervened should this have happened; indeed, Seton remained on good terms with the Drummonds. It is possible, of course, that Lillias died of a broken heart because of ill treatment or infidelity on Seton's part, but more likely giving birth five times, and perhaps being pregnant even more often, in the space of ten years was sufficient.

Lillias had died at Seton's house in Fife at Dalgety, which was his favourite residence, although the location of this building is now no longer certain. She was buried in the Seton vault at nearby St Bridget's Kirk (and where he was also buried in 1622 after dying at Pinkie House, another of his

St Bridget's Church, Dalgety.

properties). The ruins of the church are open to the public and can be visited.

Whatever the truth of her early death, within six months (in fact he was betrothed in just a few weeks), Seton had remarried, wedded to his step-niece, the young Grizel Leslie, on the 27th of October 1601.

The newly weds spent their wedding night in what is now known as the Drummond Room at Fyvie Castle. This was a night they were to remember, perhaps for the wrong reasons.

All night Seton and Grizel were disturbed by sighing and moaning coming from one of the windows, which they perhaps initially dismissed as just the wind. When it was light enough to see, however, they found the letters (as mentioned before), facing outwards, distinctly carved into the outside of the window sill, reading:

D[ame] LILLIES DRUMMOND

This must have been a little disconcerting, should it be true. A window sill, after all, facing out, is a very strange place for Lillias to have had her name carved before she was dead – or for an existing stone to be reused. Of course, that does not mean it was carved by her ghost! That the castle was believed to be haunted, however, is clear as a 'Green Ladye' is mentioned in documents dating from the seventeenth century.

Hauntings continued into the nineteenth century. The ghost was reputedly most often seen on the main stair (a maid described observing a lady she did not know in a green dress ascending the steps, not realising it was the Green Lady) but also in the corridor to the Douglas Room (or the Murder

Main stair, Fyvie Castle.

Room, as it is also known, where there are said to be blood stains).

The Green Lady is said to herald a death or misfortune in the resident family (also see the chapters on Cortachy and the MacLaines), not just the Setons, as that line became extinct, after Fyvie had been bought by the Gordons.

The ghost is said to have made her presence felt before the death of the then laird of Fyvie, Colonel Cosmo Gordon, in 1879, when he saw the apparition beckoning to him from the shadows of his chamber. Then a few days later, Cosmo's younger brother saw the ghost again, this time in the Drummond Room, when it is reported she curtseyed. Cosmo died the next day. Before that, he is reported to have been shaken out of his bed by invisible hands, and on a later occasion a great blast through the building blew the covers off several beds in which guests and family were sleeping. Alexander Gordon saw the ghost a few years later, just before his own death.

One account has the phantom being observed with a candle in its hand and pearls in its hair, and describes how it wore a green brocade dress, and emitted a soft illuminance. The Green Lady has also been reported as a shifting patch of light or as a flickering glow, witnessed often at night in one of the bedchambers.

In recent times a visitor told one of the guides, who are on hand in many of the chambers, that she had seen the phantom of a lady in the Gordon Bedroom. The presence of the ghost is also said to be heralded by the smell of roses, including during an instance in 2008 when one of the room guides witnessed the perfume and then felt as if an invisible person was pushing past them.

Grizel Leslie, Seton's new wife, herself, was also not to live into old age, and died only five years after she was married. She had three children in this brief time, and they did have a son, but he died young. Their two daughters were called Jean and Lillias.

Seton then married Margaret Hay, by whom he had several children, including Charles, who became second Earl of Dunfermline. Alexander Seton, himself, died in 1622, while Margaret Hay was to live for nearly another forty years.

The Seton Earls of Dunfermline did not survive the next generation, and James, the fourth Earl (and Alexander Seton's grandson), was forfeited in 1690, fled abroad and died four years later, without heirs and in poverty. The title became extinct and Fyvie went to the Crown, until 1733 when it was acquired by the Gordons.

Seton was buried at St Bridget's Church at Dalgety, alongside Lillias and Grizel Leslie, and later Margaret Hay and some of his children. There are a series of striking and macabre burial markers in and around the church, adorned with skulls.

Lillias's four daughters married into the noble families of Scotland: Anne, the Erskine Earls of Kellie; Isobel, the Maitland Earls of Lauderdale; Margaret, the Mackenzie Earls of Seaforth; and Sophia, the Lindsay Lords and later Earls of Balcarres.

This is not the only tale of ghosts at Fyvie.

The castle may also have a Grey or White Lady, the story going that a young woman was starved to death (anyone who tried to rescue her was slaughtered) in a secret chamber behind what is now the Gun Room. The small room was discovered when workmen were altering the building, and found her remains.

When the bones were buried, activity and disturbances became worse, and the ghost is said to have been particularly active in the 1920s and 1930s. One account describes a woman in a white flowing dress, who sailed across a room and disappeared through a door.

Manifestations apparently lessened when the remains were returned to the secret chamber and sealed within. It is possible, of course, that Lillias's manifestations and story behind her appearance and that of this Grey or White Lady have become confused.

There is also a further spooky tale about a phantom trumpeter (or a drummer, depending on the version). The story comes from around the eighteenth century. The ghost is believed to be the spirit of Andrew Lammie, who fell in love with Agnes Smith, daughter of the local miller. The match was doomed and Andrew disappeared, either sent off to Edinburgh, or sold into slavery, a disappearance in which the laird of Fyvie may have had a hand. Lammie's love wept herself into an early grave (or perhaps she was even murdered by her parents). Andrew eventually returned to Scotland, weak and ill, and found Agnes dead. Before expiring himself, he cursed the lairds of Fyvie, declaring that he would return and his trumpet would be heard, both within the walls and outside the castle, whenever one of them was near death.

And a further eerie story is that when Fyvie was first built, stones are said to have been removed from a local chapel, and some of these fell into a river. Thomas the Rhymer, the famous thirteenth-century poet and seer, tried to visit Fyvie, but he was refused entrance.

Thomas prophesied that unless three lost stones were recovered the property would never be held by the same family for more than two generations. Only two of the stones were recovered: one is in the Charter Room, while another is said to be built into in the foundations. The stones are said to weep, to ooze, when tragedy is going to occur. The stones do, or did anyway, 'weep'. This can be explained by climactic conditions as at least one of the stones is made of a porous sandstone, which absorbs and exudes water, depending on humidity.

Wrychtishousis and Bruntsfield House: Skeletons in the Closet

Two places in Edinburgh, Wrychtishousis and Bruntsfield House, are associated with James Gillespie's School – but they also both have gruesome ghost stories regarding the finding of skeletal remains concealed beneath the floor.

Nothing now remains of the castle and mansion known as Wrychtishousis, or Wrightshouses in modern parlance, which stood off what is now Gillespie Crescent in the Bruntsfield area of Edinburgh. This was an old and romantic building, part of which dated from the fourteenth century, and

Wrychtishousis.

it was embellished with numerous heraldic devices and inscriptions. For most of its history, until the 1660s, it was owned by the Napier family, but by the end of the eighteenth century was in the possession of Lieutenant General William Robertson of Lude.

Robertson was a veteran of the American War of Independence, and had served for some fifteen years before returning to Scotland when the fighting was concluded. With him, Robertson brought back a black man, known (rather unimaginatively) as Black Tom.

Tom had a bedroom on the ground floor of the old house, a chamber which had already gained a reputation for having an unpleasant atmosphere. Over the next few weeks Tom complained repeatedly that he could not sleep. This was put down to his drinking but he told a different story. On several occasions, after he had settled down for the night, he was awakened and saw the apparition of a woman, with an child in her embrace, rise from the fireplace of his chamber. This was disturbing enough in itself, but the ghost was also headless. Despite his protestations, Tom was simply not believed, his sleeplessness put down to too much alcohol causing bad dreams, and eventually he and Robertson left Wrychtishousis.

That is, of course, not quite the end of the story. The old mansion and six acres of land were sold around 1800 so that a hospital (a charitable institution to sustain old men and woman) could be built using the fortune of an Edinburgh tobacco seller, James

Gillespie. In 1802 Wrychtishousis was demolished and in its place the hospital was built (described at the time as a 'tasteless edifice'). During the demolition, skeletal remains were discovered, described thus:

> 'There was found under the hearthstone of that apartment a box containing the body of a female, from which the head had been severed, and beside her lay the remains of an infant, wrapped in a pillow-case trimmed with lace. She appeared, poor lady, to have been cut off in the blossom of her sins; for she was dressed, and her scissors were yet hanging by a ribbon to her side, and her thimble was also in the box, having, apparently, fallen from her shrivelled fingers.'

So who was the lady?

Rumours circulated that she was the wife of one of the Clerks, who gained the property in 1664. Her husband was killed in battle, leaving her young son as heir to the property. But the brother of her husband desired Wrychtishousis for himself, and murdered both the lady and his nephew, concealing his crime by disposing of their remains under the hearth.

In time James Gillespie's hospital became a school for girls and this was moved to nearby

Bruntsfield, and Edinburgh's Blind Asylum (later Royal Blind School) was established on the site of Wrychtishousis . This, too, was eventually relocated.

James Gillespie's School was set up at its new nearby site in the 1960s and the school has modern buildings surrounding the old (and to some, spooky) edifice of Bruntsfield House. The original house consists of a much-altered Z-plan building and dates from the fifteenth century. The property had several owners before it passed to the Warrender family in 1695 and they sold it in 1935 to Edinburgh Corporation. In 1880 the house had been surrounded by seventy-five acres of parkland but many of the original trees still survive around the school.

Like many old buildings, Bruntsfield House is believed to be haunted, again by a Green Lady, mostly seen (or experienced anyway) in the upper floors. One of the Warrenders, Sir George, who was an MP for the Haddington Burghs and died in 1849, made an interesting discovery about the house. One of his employees had been studying the building and realised that a count of the windows on the outside of the house did not tally with the rooms on the inside. Making further investigations, he discovered a previously unknown chamber, its entrance hidden behind an arras (or partition).

Nor was the room entirely devoid of interest, albeit in a grisly way. In the fireplace were the ashes from a fire and the floor was stained with old blood; later a skeleton was found, hidden beneath the floor under the window. Some accounts also report that

Bruntsfield House.

the remains of a child were found in the secret room.

This chamber became known as the Ghost Room, and the Green Lady is said to have been active in recent times.

Evil Spirits: Ring Croft of Stocking, Glenluce and Galdenoch

Although many seem to believe differently – and going against what some people who arrange ghost tours will tell their customers – ghosts very rarely harm the living, except perhaps by scaring them a bit. Of all the cases of hauntings in Scotland, only a handful involve any kind of physical or corporeal violence.

But there are, of course, exceptions, and three cases from the south-west of Scotland are exceptional vigorous and unpleasant manifestations of what is often called poltergeist activity. That is, the movement of objects, noises, fire raising and much else.

These cases come from the seventeenth century, a turbulent time of religious conflict, which may explain the violence of the hauntings. They were also recorded by men who had some motive in exaggerating the events, partly religious by ministers hoping to convince their congregations of the reality of evil, and partly financial by the publishers of pamphlets wanting to sell more copies.

The first case concerns Ring Croft of Stocking, a farm which once stood just to the west of the village of Auchencairn in the old county of Kirkcudbrightshire, near the present Collin Farm. The farm was occupied by Andrew Mackie, a mason and farmer, and his family in 1695.

An account of the haunting was made by the local minister, Alexander Telfair, and was issued in pamphlet form under the title: 'A True Relation of an Apparition, Expressions and Actings of a Spirit, which infested the house of Andrew Mackie in Ringcroft of Stocking, in the paroch [parish] of Rerrick, in the Stewarty of Kirkcudbright'.

The events were attested to by fifteen witnesses, including Telfair, as well as five other ministers, who all signed the original document.

The episode started in February, rather mischievously. On consecutive mornings Mackie found that his beasts had been freed from their tethers in the byre, despite tying them up carefully the previous evening – and using stronger tethers. Mackie moved the animals from the byre but then found one of the beasts tied tightly to a beam of his house. A few days later Mackie discovered a stack of peats had been piled into the middle of the dwelling and had then had been lit, although he managed to extinguish it before any damage was done. There was no obvious explanation for these odd occurrences.

Manifestations then began to escalate. From the 7th of March that year, stones were thrown at the family as they dwelt in the house, although it was impossible to determine from where these came. This was worse at night and continued for four days. On the 11th of March, while the adults were out working, the children returned to the farm to find what they thought was a shrouded figure sitting by the fire; when they removed the blanket they found only an upturned stool.

Items then went missing and the stone throwing began again, being especially bad on a Sunday. Those praying were particularly targeted.

Mackie asked the minister, Alexander Telfair, to intervene. Telfair questioned Mackie and his family regarding anything that they might have done to have angered anyone, alive or dead, but it seems that Mackie was an upright fellow and no explanation could be found. When the minister was at the farm, nothing happened until he left the house and the stone throwing began again. He went into pray and was struck himself, but then disturbances ceased until the next Sunday.

The missiles became heavier (although injuries sustained were slighter than might be expected from the weight of the stones) and the bombardment went on for nearly three days. Telfair and some of Mackie's neighbours came to pray, but the minister was struck repeatedly by rocks and was also hit on the back. Knocking was heard and the side of a box-bed was torn off. Telfair reported seeing 'a little white Hand and Arm from the elbow down, but presently it vanished'.

On several occasions the family and neighbours saw the apparition of what appeared to be a teenage lad, dressed in grey and wearing a bonnet. It is not clear, however, if this had anything to do with the haunting.

The following day things got worse again. People were hit with heavy stones and beaten with staves, until they had to leave the house. Some were dragged along the floor, others were scratched as if by fingernails. That night the children were attacked, their blankets thrown off them and then beaten about the hips as if slapped by a hand. The bar for the door moved about the room on its own, furniture shook and more stones rained down.

On the 4th of April the word 'Wisht!' was repeatedly heard when the family finished a sentence of a prayer, and whistling plagued the building. More ministers were called in, but they were hit, causing wounds and bruises, and hot peats from the fire were thrown at them.

Fires began to be lit the next day in the straw, and more and more people came from the neighbourhood to experience the manifestations: they were duly pelted with stones.

Mackie's wife disturbed a part of the floor at the threshold of the house, and found beneath it:

> 'Seven small bones, with Blood, and some Flesh, all closed in an Old suddled Paper, the Blood was fresh and bright: the sight whereof troubled her, and being afraid, laid all down again.'

The woman was much troubled by this discovery and went for advice. Meantime, the activity again intensified. Witnesses saw fireballs, although these went out before igniting anything, and a red hot stone was tossed in the children's bed and burnt through the blankets. A staff was shoved into the wall above their bed.

Eventually the bones were picked up and were taken to the minister. After returning, initially Telfair was showered with large stones – but then the activity lessened.

The next day, another Sunday, the stone throwing began again, along with movement of other heavy items. Fires were started but were put out by neighbours. One of the children was illuminated by an unearthly radiance, which followed him into the house.

The following morning Mackie found a letter outside the house. It was bedaubed in blood and appeared to accuse an unnamed resident of the house of murder. All those who had lived there were brought to the farm but no determination of guilt could be made, even after they had all touched the bones (known as a 'beirricht', a way of trying to find the culprit: if the murderer was present the remains would ooze blood).

Five ministers decided to stay in the house, along with local men, praying and fasting. They were, of course, attacked with large stones and a hole was made through the thatch of the roof and the barn door was smashed along with part of the wall. They also felt as if they a hand was clasped around the legs.

Things did not improve, not matter how much praying they did.

When a man brought a dead polecat (killed

by his dog on the way to the farm) into the house, they were all beaten with it, and a man felt as if a hand was thrust into his pocket and was so scared he vomited. A spade and a sieve were thrown about, and the whistling returned along with shouted words.

At this point, on the 16th of April, the Mackies finally left their house, although why it had taken until then seems madness on their part.

Activity diminished except for some trouble with the cattle, and when they came back little initially happened.

Within a few days, however, all hell was let loose: people were again pelted with rocks, fires were started, mud was thrown in the face of those at prayer, and people were beaten with staves. A voice also began to curse and shout at them, swearing that they were witches and rooks – and telling them they would be taken to Hell.

Mackie held a conversation with the spirit, and a voice said to him:

'God gave me a commission, and I am sent to warn you the land to repent; for a judgement is to come if the land do not quickly repent, and I will return a hundred times worse upon every family in the land.'

Then it said, 'Praise me, and I will whistle to you. Worship me, and I will trouble you no more'.

Mackie refused and the next day, a Sunday, the house was set on fire no less than seven times, although again they managed to extinguish the flames. One of the gables of the house was then demolished, and those present retired to the stable. But the violence followed them. One of the children was dragged from their resting place, and a beam was then suspended above the others, with the words,

'If I had a commission I would brain them!'

That Monday the fire raising continued, no matter that they had removed all combustible material from around the farm.

The next day, when they were praying in the barn, they saw a black shape in one corner, which grew and slowly filled the whole building, although no features could be discerned. Mud was thrown at those attending. People felt their limbs and torsos gripped by strong hands, which left an ache for days. Then the black shape faded away.

The sheep house was torched on that Wednesday and, although the flock was saved, the building was burnt out.

This was, however, the final act in a bizarre series of violent and unexplained manifestations.

Nor is there any answer, either to why the activity started or to why it so suddenly stopped.

Some forty years earlier, the house of the weaver Gilbert Campbell was plagued by similar poltergeist activity for several months in 1655. Campbell lived and worked in the village of Glenluce in Galloway, which lies about thirty-five miles to the west of Ringcroft of Stocking. The events were eventually published in *Satan's Invisible World Discovered*, some thirty years later, based on a work of 1672 called

Hydrostaticks, written by George Sinclair.

The episode seems to have begun when a beggar called Andrew Agnew came to Campbell's door, looking for charity. He was sent away without receiving anything and he cursed the family, saying that harm would come to them. This may not, of course, had anything to do with the subsequent ghostly activity, except that the manifestation suddenly stopped when Agnew was hanged.

Gilbert Campbell's young daughter, called Janet (or Jennet), started to hear shrill whistling, although others were oblivious of the noise. A neighbour heard Janet say, 'I will cast thee, Jennet, into the well,' believing that an evil spirit was speaking through her.

Like at Ringcroft of Stocking, the house was then peppered with stones. Hats, clothes and shoes were slashed and destroyed, sometimes while they were being worn by the family, and sheets and cloths were shredded. Chests were opened and their contents flung about the room. Blankets were torn from sleepers.

To keep them safe, the children were removed from the home, and unexpectedly the activity ceased. And when they returned the house remained peaceful. Until, that is, Gilbert's eldest son Thomas came back from studying in Glasgow. Then all hell broke loose again and all the violent activity restarted; the house was even set on fire.

Ministers were called in, but then could not discover the cause or the focus. A voice spoke to them, saying (among other things):

'You lie, God shall judge you for your lying, and I and my father will come and fetch you to hell with warlock thieves,' as well as telling the ministers it was 'an evil spirit come from the bottomless pit of hell to vex this house, and that Satan was his father'.

This last statement came after the voice and one of the ministers had had a contest in Biblical knowledge. A hand and arm materialised, and then hit the floor repeatedly and so hard that the whole building shook.

Manifestations became worse. The children were beaten so violently that the slaps on their buttocks reverberated (although they were apparently not actually hurt). Stones were cast, household items were moved about or hidden, and the beds were set alight.

Then as abruptly as it had begin, the activity stopped and did not return.

A similar tale surrounds Galdenoch Castle, now a ruinous tower house, which stands some miles west of Stranraer and about fifteen miles from Glenluce. Galdenoch was a property of the Agnews. The date of this episode is not certain but it is likely to be the second half of the seventeenth century. The story is recorded in *Hereditary Sheriffs of Galloway*, written by Andrew Agnew and published in 1864.

The laird of Galdenoch was a Covenanter, and finding himself pursued by Royalist forces, he took refuge at a farm, which was only inhabited by a farmer. The farmer became suspicious of the young Agnew, and tried to prevent him from leaving.

Perhaps fearing that he was to be turned over to the authorities for execution, Agnew shot the farmer, killing him. Agnew returned to Galdenoch, and no suspicion fell on him. The attack, however, was not to go unpunished and Galdenoch was apparently haunted by the vengeful spirit of the farmer.

Spinning threads were repeatedly broken, peat was put into the porridge, unpleasant stuff was mixed with food, and coals were thrown from the fire.

The most disturbing episode was when the grandmother, who had been spinning, was taken from Galdenoch and immersed in the Mill-Isle Burn, a voice apparently saying, 'I'll dip thee, I'll draw thee'. The family searched for the poor woman to no avail, until the voice told them, 'I've washed granny in the burn and laid her on the dyke to dry!' They hurried off and found her naked and shivering with the cold and fear.

Ministers were called but they could not rid the castle of the spirit. Psalms were sung but the voice sang louder and drowned out the holy men. Finally a new minister with a mighty voice was called in and he battled with the voice and this time was victorious, and the manifestations ceased. The evil spirit left, admitting defeat.

Haunted Hotels and Hostelries

Visit Scotland and other tourist rating bodies allocate stars to hotels and other accommodation based on facilities, comfort, food and a welcoming atmosphere. There is not, however, as yet a category based on supernatural encounters and hauntings. Nevertheless, many old castles and houses, inns and taverns, do have stories and legends associated with past events and ghostly sightings. Some owners even make these into unique selling points (or at least acknowledge the stories) as there are many people, either believers or sceptics, who specifically choose to stay in such places, either in an attempt to spot the 'ghost' or to prove the non-existence of the alleged spirit.

Contact details for the establishments in this section are listed in the section on the last page of this book.

Busta House Hotel, Shetland

Pronounced Boosta, Busta House Hotel is located on the north of Shetland mainland. The house, and much other property, on Shetland was owned by the Gifford family and the tragedy – which it is claimed caused ghostly apparitions and hauntings – is associated with this family.

During the eighteenth century, Thomas Gifford and his wife Elizabeth Mitchell were at the zenith of their marriage and lives. Descended from merchants and fish exporters, Gifford was Chamberlain and Steward Depute of Shetland. He and his wife had four sons and were able to extend the family house to accommodate their large family. Tragically the four young men were all drowned in a boating accident on the 14th of May 1748. The parents were left devastated, not only at the loss of their sons but also the loss of a direct male heir. It is not, however, the ghosts of any of the sons that haunt the building, but allegedly that of Barbara Pitcairn, a maid or guest at Busta.

After the drownings, it seems Barbara informed Thomas and Elizabeth that she was pregnant by one of the sons. It is claimed that she had legal paperwork to prove that she was legitimately married, but this was questioned by Thomas and Elizabeth.

When Barbara gave birth to a baby boy – named Gideon – Thomas and Elizabeth adopted him as their heir but Barbara was ostracised and forced to leave Busta. She died, in poverty, at the house of a relative in Lerwick at the age of just thirty-six. The apparition seen at Busta is said to that of a sad woman who seems to be looking for someone or something – possibly her son? Despite being accepted as Thomas' heir, Gideon did not leave any direct heirs either and later disputes and lawsuits over inheritance left the estate financially ruined.

A grey-haired lady in a brown dress and a lace cap is said to have been seen in the Linga room. If this spectre is of an older woman either Barbara aged badly or it may be the ghost of the equally tragic, although not very charitable, Elizabeth. There are other manifestations that fit the traditional model: heavy footsteps in the Foula room; lights and other electrical equipment turning off and on, apparently by themselves. Most activity is also said to occur in May, around the anniversary of the drowning of the Gifford sons, and not, apparently, on the death of Barbara which may add some weight to the suggestion that the ghost is that of the drowned men's mother.

BORTHWICK CASTLE, MIDLOTHIAN

Perhaps the most impressive and domineering stronghold in Scotland, Borthwick Castle is associated with one of the many dramatic events of the reign of Mary, Queen of Scots. After being widowed when her first husband François II, king of France, died Mary returned to Scotland in 1561. After the murder of her second husband, Henry, Lord Darnley, and her rapid and controversial marriage to James Hepburn, Earl of Bothwell, in 1567, Mary and Bothwell spent some time at Borthwick before meeting those opposed to the marriage and to Bothwell – the Confederate Lords – at Carberry Hill, near Musselburgh. It has been claimed that one of the sightings at the castle is that of Mary Queen of Scots in the guise of a pageboy. As with many other locations in Scotland (and in England) where Mary's ghost has appeared, it seems strange that her ghost would appear in more than one place rather than simply the site of her execution.

Borthwick Castle.

A much grimmer tale associated with Borthwick is that of the murder of Ann Grant. It is quite unusual for ghosts, other than those claiming to be royalty or nobility, to have a specific name. This does give the story a much greater degree of poignancy, although in this case not necessarily any greater credibility. The details of the story – poor servant/daughter who had a love affair with their master/unsuitable suitor, resulting in untimely, and often violent, death at the hands of their lover/father – are oft-repeated and to a degree typical.

Ann was a serving girl who worked in the castle and who had an affair with one of the Borthwick lairds. As with many other similar tales, the evidence of their physical relationship became apparent when Ann fell pregnant. Borthwick had Ann attacked and she was slashed across the stomach, killing both Ann and her baby; she was left to die in her own blood. The apparition and other manifestations – changes in temperature, footsteps in the turnpike stair, sobbing, wailing, doors opening by themselves – are said to have been witnessed by a former owner of the castle – Helen Bailey – and by other visitors.

The Red Room is said to be where the murder took place and the apparition is more of a tableau – a vision of the murder – than simply a shade of the victim. A female figure being held by two other women while a 'soldier' (although why a soldier?) cuts her across the abdomen.

A third ghostly apparition associated with Borthwick is more mundane and is said to be that of a chancellor of the castle who, after being caught embezzling money, was burnt to death. This was an unusual form of execution for theft, more often associated with heresy or witchcraft, and it may not have been state sanctioned, which may account for the unsettled spirit.

AIRTH CASTLE, AIRTH

Negligent nanny searching for children: this is the basis for the alleged sad story behind the ghostly activities claimed to have been seen or felt in some of the rooms in Airth Castle. The story's origins are from the seventeenth century, when a nursemaid or housekeeper did not manage to safe the lives of two children when the castle was engulfed by fire.

The manifestations seem to be sounds of children playing, as well as an apparition of a woman who seems to be looking for someone or something, but other unspecified 'ghostly' activity has been reported in various parts of the hotel.

THUNDERTON HOUSE, ELGIN

The romance and myth of the Jacobite cause: Bonnie Prince Charlie, Flora MacDonald, misty moor hens, the sweet scent of heather crushed beneath the feet of marching men, dramatic escapes wearing the clothes of servants, brave deaths for a just and noble cause. The truth is, as ever, a darker and harsher reality: questionable military tactics, egotism, bad timing, cruel and violent deaths and punishment, and ultimate abandonment.

Charlie's no coming back again, but his ghost apparently has never left some places. Thunderton House is one such lucky site. Charlie stayed at Thunderton for some days before advancing to the less than glorious defeat at Culloden Moor in the spring of 1746. There is, however, an alternative theory: that the apparition is that of Lady Arradoul, whose shroud was seemingly made from the sheets that were used by Charlie during his visit: perhaps, going by Charlie's well-known reputation as a bit of a lady's man, the sheets were witness to a particular kind of nocturnal activity…

The disturbances are said to include the sound of the bagpipes – Charlie was said to have enjoyed pipe music – and voices, in addition to objects being moved around the rooms.

CULLODEN HOUSE, CULLODEN

Like Thunderton House, Culloden House is also said to be haunted by Bonnie Prince Charlie, although why he should chose to haunt a location associated with his opponents is strange. Duncan Forbes of Culloden fought with the Hanoverians and the Duke of Cumberland, younger son of George II. The Duke of Cumberland, William Augustus, was a man of many epithets: Butcher, Stinking Willie or Sweet William, and Culloden House was where injured Jacobites were brought after the battle and there were summarily executed, without trial, for being 'rebellious Scots'.

Culloden House.

The ghost is said to be that of a man in tartan and, while Bonnie Prince Charlie was not averse to wearing a bit of plaid, so did most of his supporters, so it is just as likely that the apparition could be of one of the prince's unfortunate army. There is more cachet, however, in having an apparition of Prince Charlie who died in his bed a drunken, debauched, disappointed man, than that of an anonymous Jacobite foot-soldier violently executed for following orders and misplaced loyalty.

COMLONGON CASTLE, COMLONGON

Marriage was rarely a meeting of hearts and minds in the past, especially if the bride came from a family with land and even more so if, according to Scots law, she was heir to wealthy estates and property. One such lass was Marion Carruthers, whose spirit – a ghost in green – is said to haunt Comlongon Castle, now part of a hotel.

In 1548 Marion Carruthers of Mouswald's father, Sir Simon Carruthers, was killed in battle and Marion and her sister, Janet, stood to inherit the property. Marion was forced into a marriage to John MacMath of Dalpeddar, nephew of her guardian Sir James Douglas of Drumlanrig or possibly to Sir James himself. It is likely that the attraction for both MacMath, and her guardian, was her potential wealth, as on her marriage her property would pass to her husband. Marion, however, objected and refused to marry MacMath.

After many years, a possible period of imprisonment at Hermitage, and the ultimate

Comlongon Castle.

involvement of the privy council, Marion was ordered in to the care of Borthwick Castle in Midlothian in 1563, to await a final decision.

Marion did not go to Borthwick and instead sought refuge at Comlongon which belonged to her uncle Sir William Murray, who might have been a better choice of guardian.

It was at Comlongon that Marion died in September 1570 when she was around twenty-nine years old. One explanation for her death was that she was so worn down by all the protracted disputes that she committed suicide by jumping from the tower: 'she did wilfully take her own life by leaping from the lookout tower' and 'did break her head and bones'. Another, more sinister, version was that she was murdered by the Douglases in revenge for all the problems she had caused. It is said that no grass grows on the spot where her body fell and that, since the official account of her death recorded death by suicide, she was refused a Christian burial. Douglas did well out of her death and inherited her share of her father's property; MacMath would appear to have got nothing.

A green spectre of a sad, weeping female has been witnessed in the grounds and in the castle itself, as well as reports of sounds of crying although with no apparition: Marion's spirit, it might seem, is seeking restitution and a proper burial. Other reports claim that people have experienced a force or ghostly presence pushing past them and there have been a few recent sightings, including in a photograph which allegedly shows her ghost.

DREADNOUGHT HOTEL, CALLANDER

'Dread Nought' is the motto of the clan MacNab and one of the chiefs, Francis MacNab of Kinnell House, near Killin, chief of the MacNabs, is depicted in Henry Raeburn's portrait in full Highland dress, the very epitome of a Highland laird. His private life was, however, less salubrious or successful, as he left his heir, his nephew Archibald, only debts. His legacy to the hotel was no less impressive as he was associated with, or indeed allegedly was the cause of, ghostly manifestations.

MacNab built the Dreadnought in Callander as a hotel in 1802 and it is claimed that it is haunted by the spirit of a young woman, with both explanations of her demise related to the erstwhile Highland chief. The first is that he had made a young servant girl pregnant and when he found out he flung her out one of the windows. The other is that she is the ghost of his wife whom he walled up in one of the rooms.

Another reputed ghostly occurrence has manifested itself with sobs and cries, emanating from one of the bedrooms. These are the cries of a child, rather than a grown woman, and stories claim that MacNab drowned one of his illegitimate offspring in an old well in the basement of the hotel. A third manifestation is that of a male ghost, which it is claimed is the ghost of MacNab himself, a somewhat appropriate punishment if the other stories are true.

COYLET INN, NEAR DUNOON

Another hotel which claims to have a child ghost is the Coylet Inn (originally the Loch Eck Inn). The story

Coylet Inn.

is a poignant one and illustrates every parent's nightmare: children sleepwalking to their deaths. A young boy, who it was claimed had a history of sleep walking, was staying at the inn and during the night appears to have walked down to the loch and drowned; his cold, blue body was found sometime later. The manifestations seem to reflect the condition of his corpse, as staff have reported seeing wet footsteps on the floor. The 'Blue Boy' activity is particularly associated with Room 4 and it is thought that the sprit is returning to look for his mother. Objects have also disappeared and reappeared from time to time; perhaps reflecting a more playful aspect to this child ghost?

DORNOCH CASTLE HOTEL, DORNOCH

Sheep stealing was not an uncommon crime, especially during times of hardship, of which there were many in the Highlands in the nineteenth century, when many families and communities were cleared off their lands to make way for sheep and deer. It was however a serious crime and one for which the culprit could be hanged and Andrew McCornish was one such individual. He was imprisoned in Dornoch Castle when it was used as a courthouse and jail in the nineteenth century and it has been claimed that his apparition was seen during the late 1800s. Other manifestations of his somewhat angry spirit have included shaking walls, strange noises, and the sounds of furniture being dragged across the floor. Whilst it is possible McCornish must have felt extremely aggrieved at his sentence, he must surely have not been the only one who committed this crime, so it is not entirely clear why the ghost is thought to be associated with McCornish. Maybe he was innocent? Maybe he felt that circumstances beyond his control had reduced him to such a state that stealing a sheep was his last option? Maybe he blamed the good and the godly in the town for his poverty? It does seem that his ghost is not at peace.

GALLOWAY ARMS HOTEL, CROCKETFORD

Elizabeth Buchan is said to haunt the old coaching inn here. She died in 1791 and her spirit would appear to be restless for a very particular reason. She was not murdered horribly or raped, she did not commit suicide, she did not lose a child, nor was she killed accidentally. On the contrary, it would seem that she died in her bed of natural causes. But , then again, Elizabeth's religious beliefs about the afterlife may have been something of a disappointment for her once she died.

Elizabeth started a religious sect in 1787 called – not very originally – the Buchanites, after claiming she had experienced religious visions. There are a number of related contextual factors that demonstrate Elizabeth's behaviour was not that unusual. The eighteenth century was a time of much religious awakening and there were several schisms within the Church of Scotland, resulting in a number of, sometimes quite small, breakaway groups and sects. The Church of Scotland also had no official role for women – other than being the wife of a minister – and undoubtedly this must have been frustrating for women who felt they had a spiritual or religious message to convey. The third factor was that Elizabeth's beliefs related to Apocalyptic visions, which regularly provoke anxieties in the couple of decades before the end of a century.

Elizabeth claimed that she was the re-embodiment of a character from the Book of Revelation in *The Bible*, the main focus of which is describing, in detail, the end of the world and the Day of Judgement. She must also have been quite a successful preacher or inspiring speaker as it is claimed she attracted a large following, who lived together in Crocketford in the building which is now the Galloway Arms Hotel. The fundamental belief of the Buchanites was that they would ascend to heaven without dying. It is not clear if this was all to happen on one appointed day, but clearly Elizabeth's death must have been a bit frustrating for her as she may either have died too soon or her visions were incorrect. Support for the Buchanites seems to have withered following her untimely departure.

Her unsettled ghost reportedly still haunts the building – possibly still looking for a way to heaven?

DROVERS INN, INVERARNAN

The cattle trade was one of the mainstays of the Highland economy and transporting beasts on the hoof to the markets in the south was often a long and arduous journey. Drovers' inns, which provided shelter, accommodation and refreshment, were a welcome sight and were found all over the country.

Many are still extant today and are still used as inns or hotels. Although a drover is claimed to be the origin of one of the ghostly apparitions experience at the Drovers Inn at Inverarnan, other manifestations have also been reported.

Several people who have spent the night in Room 6 reported that they have woken up in the middle of the night feeling as if a damp and cold body is lying next to them in the bed. The origin of the explanation is that a young girl drowned – there is no reference to it being anything other than an

Drovers Inn, Inverarnan.

accident – in a nearby river, the River Falloch, and her corpse was brought to the hotel and laid out in that particular room to await burial.

The story of Angus, the cattle drover's ghost, is an everyday tale of eighteenth-century inter-clan rivalry, theft and murder, likely one of many similar events. It is said he arrived at the inn for rest and refreshment after a long trip. Rather carelessly, he overindulged in a few too many whiskies and overslept the next morning. His herd of cattle was stolen in the middle of the night by a rival clan, not an entirely unusual event.

Angus clearly had some responsibility for events, as he should presumably have been aware that cattle reiving was rife and any livestock needed to be guarded. He had to return to his clan chief with no cattle and no money and, in punishment, his family was killed – to which clan Angus belonged is not recorded – and he was left to seek his own revenge on the thieves. He went to the inn and waited for them to return but, according to legend, they attacked him first and murdered him by hanging him from a tree behind the inn. The ghostly apparition is apparently that of a searching figure, screaming and wandering around the hallways of the building, presumably looking for revenge. For the thieves got off with both stealing the cattle and with his murder.

The provenance of the ghosts in Room 2 is linked to 1792 and the 'Year of the Sheep': an instance of people being removed from their croft land to make way for the more economical sheep. A young family – husband, wife and son – had nowhere to live and no means to earn a living and so headed south for some hope of employment. Unfortunately their journey was during the winter months and it is said that they lost their way trying to find the shelter of the Drovers Inn and froze to death. There have been reports over the years of people claiming to have seen a family group wandering around the area during the winter. Other versions report that people have been woken by the cold in Room 2 to see the apparitions of the family standing at the end of the bed – perhaps looking for the shelter they never found?

There have been several other ghostly sightings reported at the Drovers Inn, including that of an ancient bar regular 'Old George', whose ashes are apparently kept in an urn at the inn.

Another odd, and slightly strange story, is that a couple, staying overnight at the inn, found photographs of them sleeping in bed in their camera. While there might be a supernatural explanation of some inquisitive spiritual visitor, it could also be that there was a more obvious and corporeal visitor to their room – the moral of this tale is make sure you lock your door at night!

The Ghostly Cannon Ball of Caroline Park House

Perhaps one of the most bizarre hauntings in Scotland is that recorded in the 1850s at Caroline Park House in the Granton area of Edinburgh. Here a ghostly cannon ball smashed in through one of the windows of the house, seen on at least two occasions, and heard far more often.

Caroline Park House is now a fine courtyard mansion but it incorporates an old tower house of 1585, when the property was known as Royston. By the middle of the nineteenth century, the house and estate was owned by the Dukes of Buccleuch. Caroline Park was the residence of Lord John Montague-Douglas Scott, a younger son of the fourth Duke, and by his wife Alicia Ann Spottiswoode. Alicia was a songwriter and composer, and wrote the music to the famous song 'Annie Laurie' in 1838.

One night, around 11.00 pm, Alicia was in the Aurora Room of Caroline Park. Without warning the window burst open with a huge crash, and a cannon ball was catapulted through it, bounced three times along the floor, and then came to rest at the foot of a draught-screen. Alicia was undoubtedly perturbed and rang the bell for the servants to come. But, by the time they arrived, the window was closed and the cannon ball had vanished. It is not clear what reaction this invoked in Alicia or how she explained her behaviour to her staff.

Caroline Park House.

Some might argue, indeed, that Alicia had drifted off into a doze and had dreamt the whole episode. In 1879, however, the same thing happened to a governess, who was alone in the Aurora Room, and again the cannon ball vanished after bouncing along the floor.

There are not any other reports of the cannon ball being observed, but there are of it being repeatedly heard, so that the strange manifestation almost became commonplace.

No explanation has been forthcoming to explain the phenomenon, either a corporeal or a ghostly one. Although a fortified building, Caroline Park was ever attacked, never mind bombarded with cannon, so the whole episode remains doubly mysterious.

The house is also said to be haunted by a Green Lady, the ghost of Lady Royston, wife of Sir James

Mackenzie, younger son of Lord Tarbat. On certain days, her phantom, which is clad in an emerald-green gown covered with mystic devices, is reported to appear at midnight from an old well, and float over to the entrance of the house, where it vanishes. The apparition is said to then reappear in the small courtyard and ring an old bell.

The grandniece of Alicia, Margaret Warrender, reported often hearing the bell tolling of its own volition deep at night, even when there was (apparently) nobody about and not a breath of wind to stir even a cobweb.

Edinburgh's Dark Underside

Edinburgh makes much of its reputation to attract visitors from all over the world: the Castle and the Gardens; Holyrood Palace and the Holyrood Parliament; art galleries and museums; festivals and fringes; restaurants and bars; music and theatre, history and literature, and ghosts ... not one or two but scores: men, women and children; tinkers, tailors, soldiers, sailors, rich men, poor men, beggar men, thief; butchers, bakers, candlestick makers and even dog or two!

This list may not be absolutely accurate but it is not that far removed from the numerous ghost stories associated with the city, some of the most ghastly of which are found not above ground but underneath the bustling streets, shops and houses of the capital.

BLAIR STREET VAULTS

Wandering through the Grassmarket or Cowgate parts of Edinburgh late at night, you may well be greeted by the sight of people falling out of pubs, singing, dancing, or shouting insults – depending on how 'successful' their evening has been. This is usually the result of an overabundance of hormones, post-exam celebration, post-rugby/football consolation, or even just a let-off-steam after work, and most of the participants may well feel a bit ghostly-white the day after the night before.

'Mr Boots', a phantom clad in a long blue frock coat and leather boots, it would seem is forever in this condition. His spectre, dressed in late-eighteenth or nineteenth century attire, is a grumpy old ghost seen in the Blair Street vaults. He has reportedly whispered obscenities – he seems to be one of the very few talking spirits – whilst blocking doorways and smelling strongly of whisky.

There does not seem to be any origin story or

Blair Street Vaults.

explanation about why his spectre would appear here. The Blair Street Vaults, and other vaults under Edinburgh's South Bridge, were used at various times as taverns, workshops, storage, homes, hiding places, escape routes, and the area is now a focus for several ghosts and bogles. Seemingly, 'Mr Boots' resents mortals disturbing his peace and quiet.

There are reputedly at least nine different apparitions haunting Blair Street, including 'Mr Boots', but they are not all as unwelcoming or grumpy. 'Jack', a young lad, seemingly helps put on visitors' coats and jackets: maybe he's still looking for a tip. Another man simply watches; he is said to have been a cobbler. Pregnant women have reported seeing a 'Lady in Black'; perhaps she is jealous or perhaps she is simply concerned? There have also been sightings of a man in a cloak and top hat, very a la mode; an old woman; a ghostly, but not howling, hound and, somewhat intriguingly, an apparition of a naked man floating under the roof.

Other ghostly motifs have been reported here as well: the sensation of breath on the back of people's necks; voices; footsteps; growling; smells; stones being thrown; the sounds of dragging furniture and changes in temperature; lights and torches going out and the sensation of being pushed or jostled – presumably not by the people rushing to leave having experienced all of the above!

NIDDRY STREET VAULTS
The vaults here have a similar history to those in Blair Street. Located under South Bridge, which

spans the Cowgate, these vaults were part of the many tenements built on each side. They were used for storage, workshops and even dwellings but, apart from use as shelters from air attacks during World War II, they were mostly abandoned for decades.

Whatever spirits and spectres inhabited the rooms were left to their own devices, minding their own business and not disturbing anyone. Once the vaults were reopened and renovated in the 1990s they have presumably been stirred into activity. Perhaps they, too, resent that their peace has been destroyed by party-goers, inquisitive visitors, people attempting to worship ancient deities, or those who deliberately wish to provoke spirits of any kind.

The alleged unfriendly poltergeist in these vaults is said to mostly attack female visitors, particularly in one of the larger chambers. The attacks have resulted in cuts, scratches and bruising. Those who have visited the room using cameras and torches and other electrical equipment, to try and capture images or sightings, have reported that their apparatus was damaged or lost power; it would seem that this spirit is a bit camera shy…

One of the other rooms, it is claimed, is the site of a pagan temple, which consists of a circle of stones on the floor. It is reported that the site has been long-since disused because of 'bad things' and anyone stepping inside the circle will be inviting ill luck. It is not clear why this spot should have been a pagan temple and how this has been proved, but it would seem that pagan ghostly spirits can be just as unpleasant as their Christian counterparts.

MARY KING'S CLOSE

Further up the High Street, towards the Castle, lies Mary King's Close. Although located underneath the present City Chambers, this was once a street of tenements, some of which were up to seven storeys high. The close is another of Edinburgh's spooky sites, with many tales of various ghostly apparitions and experiences.

The particular historical event which gives rise to the most commonly accepted origin relates to an outbreak of plague. Plague or Black Death was a frequent worry for town communities, and Edinburgh was no exception, experiencing several outbreaks from 1513 onwards.

The worst episode was in 1645 and claimed many victims, some put the figure at half the population. Because the town was so overcrowded and dirty, the conditions were perfect both for the infestation to thrive and for the infection to spread. By 1645 the town council was quite aware of the effects of such an outbreak and did employ two doctors to treat the infected: John Paulitious and George Rae. Paulitious died of the disease shortly after starting work, but Rae survived and seemingly then had to pursue the council for non-payment of his salary; presumably they had expected him to die as well thus saving some money.

In 1645 the council also decided to close off and seal Mary King's close, as the residents in the street had been particularly badly hit by the disease. This meant leaving those who still lived in the buildings to their fate: it was unlikely that they would survive. The tenements were left empty for several years but later, because of increased pressure on the limited housing available in the Old Town, the council opened up the close and the buildings. Presumably they had previously cleared the area of corpses. It seems, however, that the new residents did not find their new accommodation very pleasant, as the spirits of the previous occupants were not very welcoming. The newcomers reported apparitions of disembodied men and headless animals, although what the decapitated animals had to do with death by plague is unclear. The close was eventually abandoned and later the top levels were demolished and the remaining lower storeys were left underneath the City Chambers. Cynics might suggest that the residents who were housed in the close after the events of 1645 may have used stories about hauntings and ghosts in the hope of being offered alternative housing.

One of the spirits is said to be that of a child, and she has been given the name 'Annie'. Annie has been seen and felt in one particular room, and seemingly is around five or six, and wears a dirty, torn dress. Visitors leave toys in the room, perhaps as a peace offering, although a little too late if she really was one of the plague victims. Another vision that has been seen is that of an old lady dressed in black. It is not clear if her clothing is in the style worn in seventeenth-century Edinburgh. There are also claims about other typical ghostly manifestations, such as temperature changes, cameras not working and so on …

The Starving Spectre
of Spedlins

Arson and starvation are the key features behind the reasons for the supposed haunting of Spedlins Tower in Dumfries and Galloway. It is another legend that is given some more credibility as it has named characters and recorded factual events.

The owner of the lands and tower of Spedlins during the mid-seventeenth century was Sir Alexander Jardine. One of his tenants, a miller by the name of James 'Dunty' Porteous, had set his cottage or mill on fire (the reason he did so has not been preserved) and, having power of jurisdiction in the area, Jardine took Dunty prisoner and had him incarcerated in the pit prison of tower.

These chambers were well named for they were dark, windowless dungeons, deep under the floors of a castle, and usually entered only by means of a trapdoor.

While Dunty was still in the pit, Jardine left to attend to some business in Edinburgh and was away for some time. Unfortunately for the poor miller, accidentally or on purpose, Jardine took the key to the door with him and also appears not to have left anyone in charge of the prisoner. Or possibly Jardine's wife, Margaret Douglas, chose to ignore the fact that there was a prisoner who would cost money to care for and feed. On his return, Jardine found Porteous dead, having died of hunger – but not before the miller had bitten and chewed both his hands and feet. This was probably more of an attempt to free himself of his manacles than to assuage his hunger pangs. Porteous's death has been graphically described thus: '... the dying man was so ravaged by hunger he had gnawed at his own hands and feet in the last throes of torment'.

But that was not the end of the story. Indeed Jardine and his family paid the price of his neglect – or maybe it was Jardine's guilty conscience?

Whatever reason, it was claimed that Porteous's spirit then started haunting Spedlins. Lots of different kinds of supernatural activity was reported: shrieking, banging, battering, a voice shouting, 'Let me out ... I'm dying of hunger ...'

The Jardines tried numerous exorcisms but to no avail, finally after enduring several years of haunting, it seemed that Porteous's angry ghost was

Spedlins Tower (before restoration).

eventually quietened when a bible was left near the door to the dungeon. The family then also decanted to nearby Jardine Hall, a far more comfortable residence – even without the unfortunate bogle.

If the bible was moved, however, the ghostly activity would start up again. In 1710 the bible was taken away for repair and it is claimed the ghost then pursued that particular generation of Jardines in their new family mansion. The laird and his wife were thrown out of their bed and other sorts of commotion occurred – until the bible was replaced.

Once Spedlins Tower became ruinous, rumours began that the spectre of a tall man with white hair and no hands, had been seen in what was the basement or dungeon of the tower. There were also reports that if sticks were put through the door to the prison, the bark would be stripped and chewed, as if the ghost had tried to eat them.

Spedlins Tower has now been restored and reoccupied, but there have been no reports of further supernatural activity. The bible no longer rests at the entrance to the dungeon at Spedlins, but seemingly the Jardines kept it for generations (it is now preserved in a local museum) presumably just in case Porteous decided to come after the family again, wherever they were – or are ...

A Haunted Swimming Pool: Renfrew Victory Baths

There is no doubt that swimming can be a healthy past-time; it stretches and tones muscles, improves lung capacity, builds stamina – although there are relatively few people, other than competitive swimmers, who can swim non-stop for up to four hours a day. As an exercise it can be both relaxing and revitalising at the same time.

It can also lead to the occasional death by drowning.

Most swimming pools are not haunted by the spectres of drowned people; if they were it might be bad for business. Indeed most swimming pools have, fortunately, not experienced many drownings but at least two apparitions have been reported at the Victory Baths in Renfrew, although only one seems to be directly associated with the swimming pool.

In the 1920s after World War I, acquiring German army gear was regarded as a bit of a status symbol for the allies.

The story is that an unfortunate young lad had decided to wear a German army helmet, (which presumably he had been given as a gift from some male relative after the war), while he was swimming in the baths and, more seriously, while he was diving from the boards. It is thought that when he dived off the highest board, the helmet pulled his head back and broke his neck: it is not clear if the injury was sustained during the dive or when he hit the water, but whatever the cause it proved fatal, and poor lad was killed.

His apparition has reportedly been seen in recent years and, even, allegedly captured by one of the wonders of the modern world: the mobile phone. A member of staff reputedly saw an apparition of the boy walking along the floor and then floating

Renfrew Victory Baths.

up towards the viewing gallery, and the event was recorded on the mobile phone.

The second ghost is believed to be that of a white lady, and there does not seem to be any suggestion that she drowned, as her apparition is not seen in, or near the pool itself, but in storage rooms below. She has been observed on several occasions, wearing a white, floaty dress, and to be visible for several seconds but, unlike the diving boy, there are no clues as to why she might haunt the building or what happened to her.

Her apparition, like her story, will probably remain a mystery.

The Many Ghosts of Glamis Castle

Glamis Castle is a magnificent castle and stately home, but it is probably best known, perhaps a little unfairly, for its multitude of ghosts rather than the magnificence of the building. The huge tower of Glamis has walls up to fifteen-foot thick and a stair of one hundred and forty-three steps. Glamis is mentioned in Shakespeare's *Macbeth*, but any association (as Cawdor) with the present castle is from the play as Glamis is not mentioned in records or histories until 1264. The castle and lands have been held since the fourteenth century by the Lyon family, now Bowes-Lyon, Earls of Strathmore and of Kinghorne. Elizabeth Bowes-Lyon, who died in 2002,

Glamis Castle.

sprang from the family and was the present Queen's mother.

There are many ghost stories associated with Glamis. These include the apparition of a little African servant boy; a White Lady said to be seen in an avenue of trees which leads up to the castle; the ghost of a butler who hanged himself; the bogle of a tongueless woman; a phantom party of Ogilvys sealed up in a secret room at Glamis; and the spirit of a servant girl who was purported to be a vampire and drained a victim white before being walled up.

One of the most famous stories regards another sealed and abandoned chamber, where the shades of several men, including 'Earl Beardie', are said to be trapped forever playing cards with the Devil. It is not clear whether the main protagonist was Patrick Lyon, first Lord Glamis, who died in 1459 and may have been known as 'Earl Beardie', or Alexander Lindsay, fourth Earl of Crawford, who was definitely known as 'Earl Beardie', one of Lord Glamis's contemporaries.

The story goes that the party is compelled to play until the 'day of doom' for gambling on the Sabbath and making a wager with the Devil that resulted in losing their souls. The Earl of Crawford (one story is that his own dear mother smothered her own brother so that he would succeed to the title) was certainly a cruel and ruthless character, although Patrick Lyon was reputedly little better.

One detail is that as the game progressed, a servant put his eye to the keyhole of the door – and was forever blinded in that eye.

The story then goes that such disturbance and noise issued from the chamber that eventually it was locked up and people feared to enter there This did not, however, entirely solve the problem and unexplained sounds still plagued Glamis.

The following comes from a book of 1875, called *Glimpses of the Supernatural*:

> 'There is no doubt about the reality of the noises at Glamis Castle. On one occasion, some years ago, the head of the family, with several companions, was determined to investigate the cause. One night, when the disturbance was greater and more violent than usual, and it should be premised strange, weird and unearthly sounds had often been heard, and by many persons, some quite unacquainted with the ill repute of the Castle, his lordship went to the haunted room, opened the door with a key, and dropped back in a dead swoon into the arms of his companions; nor could he ever be induced to open his lips on the subject afterwards.'

A further excerpt from that work may be related, also believed to be associated with 'Earl Beardie':

> 'A lady and her child were staying for a few days at the Castle. The child was

asleep in an adjoining dressing room, and the lady, having gone to bed, lay awake for a while. Suddenly a cold blast stole into the room, extinguishing the night light by her bedside, but not affecting the one in the dressing-room beyond, in which her child had its cot. By that light she saw a tall mailed figure pass into the dressing-room from that in which she was lying. Immediately thereafter there was a shriek from the child. Her maternal instinct was aroused. She rushed into the dressing-room and found the child in agony of fear. It described what it had seen as giant who came and leant over its face.'

This is apparently not the only time that this had happened: other children staying in the upper rooms of the castle reportedly woke to find a huge bearded phantom leaning over the beds and observing them.

Another story regards Lady Janet Douglas, the beautiful widow of John Lyon, sixth Lord Glamis. Janet had a son by John (also called John), and later married Walter Campbell of Skipness. She was also the sister of Archibald Douglas, fifth Earl of Angus, and was hated, along with the rest of her family, by James V. James had been ill treated and imprisoned in his youth by the Earl of Angus, who had also married his mother, Margaret Tudor, after the death of his father James IV at the disastrous battle of

Flodden in 1513. The Earl of Angus virtually ruled the kingdom. James V eventually escaped his clutches and asserted his rule. And, although James besieged the outlawed Earl of Angus in Tantallon Castle in 1528, the Earl fled and escaped his clutches: Janet was not to be so lucky.

Janet, who was about thirty-two at the time, was accused of treasonably communicating with her exiled brother (which she may well have done) but she failed to appear on this charge. The king's forces then besieged Glamis and Janet was seized, along with her son and husband. All three were brought to Edinburgh Castle and there imprisoned for weeks in a dark pit.

Janet was then also charged with both trying to poison the king and of being a witch, accusations which were undoubtedly false. The young woman, of good and upright character, defended herself eloquently, but it was to no avail: she was burned alive (punishment for treason) on Castle Hill in Edinburgh on the 3rd of December 1537. She had been imprisoned with her husband and her son John for so long that she had nearly gone blind. Her family was forced to watch the execution.

One description of her says:

> 'She was in the prime of her life, of a singular beauty, and suffering through all, though a woman, with a man-like courage.'

Glamis was forfeited to the Crown, and John,

her orphaned son, was also sentenced to death, although he was too young at the time for the execution to proceed.

Her husband Walter tried to escape from the castle but fell down the rock and was killed. Luckily for her son John, James V died in 1542 and John was pardoned. He went on to inherit his father's property, including Glamis Castle, although the castle had been ransacked and looted by the king's men.

Janet's ghost is said to haunt the spot where she died on the esplanade outside Edinburgh Castle, but also reputedly returned to Glamis. The story is that her apparition, known as the Grey Lady (although possibly also the White Lady; however this may be an entirely different ghost), has reputedly been seen in the castle chapel as well as in the clock tower. Glamis Castle is open to the public and the chapel may be visited.

Hammering and banging, believed to come from her execution, are also said to plague the building. One account of 1880 relates:

> 'A lady, well known in London Society, an artistic and social celebrity, wealthy beyond all doubts of the future, and what is called very cultivated and instructed, but clear-headed, and perhaps slightly matter-of-fact woman, went to stay at Glamis Castle for the first time. She was allotted very handsome apartments, just on the point of the junction between the new buildings –

perhaps a hundred or two hundred years old – and the very ancient part of the castle. The rooms were handsomely furnished: no gaunt carvings grinned from the walls; no grim tapestry swung to and fro, making strange figures look the stranger by the flickering firelight; all was smooth, cosy, and modern, and the guest retired to bed without a thought of the mysteries of Glamis. In the morning she appeared at the breakfast-table quite cheerfully and self-possessed. To the inquiry how she had slept, she replied: 'Well, thanks, very well, up to four o'clock in the morning. But your Scottish carpenters seem to come to work very early. I suppose they put up their scaffolding quickly, though, for they are quiet now.' This speech produced a dead silence, and the speaker saw with astonishment that the faces of members of the family were very pale.

She was asked, as she valued the friendship of all there, never to speak to them on the subject again; there had been no carpenters at Glamis Castle for months past. This fact, whatever it may be worth, is absolutely established, so far as the testimony of a single witness can establish anything. The lady was awakened by a loud knocking and hammering, as if somebody were putting up a scaffold, and the noise did not alarm her in the least. On the contrary, she took it for an accident, due to the presumed matutinal [morning] habits of the people. She knew, of course, there were stories about Glamis, but had not the remotest idea that the hammering she had heard was connected with any story.'

One sunny day, Lady Granville, the aunt of the then Earl and sister to the Queen Mother, saw the ghost in the chapel, kneeling at one of the pews. She could see the figure and dress quite clearly but the sun shone through the ghost, making a pattern on the floor. Timothy Patrick, the sixteenth Earl of Strathmore, also saw the Grey Lady at a different time, kneeling in the chapel, and he then withdrew and left her alone. A further detail is that a guide taking visitors round the castle noticed that people visiting the chapel never sat on one particular pew, as if it was already occupied.

A further account has the Grey Lady being seen on the day that James 'the Old Pretender' visited the chapel at Glamis in January 1716 to cure the King's Evil (or scrofula, as it is also known). The Grey Lady was observed, entering the chapel and then kneeling in prayer. Of course, James was the great great great grandson of James V, the man who had had Janet Douglas so horribly and unjustly executed.

Contact details for sites which can be visited are listed below, in the order they appear in the text.

Cortachy Castle, Angus
Castle NOT open; garden open once a year.
www.gardensofscotland.org / 01575 570108

Fyvie Castle, Aberdeenshire
www.nts.org.uk / 0844 493 2182

Busta House Hotel, Shetland
www.bustahouse.com / 01806 522506

Borthwick Castle, Midlothian
www.borthwickcastle.com 01875 820514

Airth Castle Hotel, Falkirk
www.airthcastlehotel.com / 01324 831411

Thunderton House, Elgin
www.thundertonhouse.co.uk / 01343 554920

Culloden House, Highland
www.cullodenhouse.co.uk / 01463 790461

Comlongon Castle, Dumfries
www.comlongon.com / 01387 870283

Dreadnought Hotel, Callander
www.oxfordhotelsandinns.com 08444 146534

Coylet Inn, Loch Eck, Argyll
www.coyletinn.co.uk / 01369 840426

Dornoch Castle Hotel, Dornoch
www.dornochcastlehotel.com / 01862 810216

Galloway Arms Hotel, Crocketford
www.gallowayarmshotel.co.uk 01556 690248

Drovers Inn, Inverarnan
www.thedroversinn.co.uk / 01301 704234

Blair Street Vaults
www.mercattours.com / 0131 225 5445

Niddry Street Vaults
www.auldreekietours.com / 0131 557 4700

Mary King's Close
www.realmarykingsclose.com / 0845 070 6244

Glamis Castle
www.glamis-castle.co.uk / 01307 840393

Sites in this list are open to the public, either as visitor attractions or as hotels or hostelries.